Penguins

written and photographed
by Lynn M. Stone

EARLY BIRD NATURE BOOKS

Lerner Publications Company • Minneapolis, Minnesota

For Lynda, whose support made possible my penguin summer.

Thanks to our series consultant, Sharyn Fenwick, elementary science/math specialist. Mrs. Fenwick was the winner of the National Science Teachers Association 1991 Distinguished Teaching Award. She also was the recipient of the Presidential Award for Excellence in Math and Science Teaching, representing the state of Minnesota at the elementary level in 1992.

Additional photographs are reproduced through the courtesy of: © Wolfgang Kaehler, pp. 7, 17, 28, 30, 37; © Kjell B. Sandved/Visuals Unlimited, p. 25.

Early Bird Nature Books were conceptualized by Ruth Berman and designed by Steve Foley. Series editor is Joelle Goldman.

Website address: www.lernerbooks.com

Library of Congress Cataloging-in-Publication Data

Stone, Lynn M.
    Penguins / written and photographed by Lynn M. Stone.
    p. cm. — (Early bird nature books)
    Includes index.
    ISBN 0-8225-3022-8 (alk. paper)
    1. Penguins—Juvenile literature.   I. Title. II. Series.
QL696.S473S75 1998
598.47—dc21   97-51933

Manufactured in the United States of America
1 2 3 4 5 6 – SP – 03 02 01 00 99 98

Contents

Map 5

Be a Word Detective 5

Chapter 1 **Penguins Are Special Birds** 6

Chapter 2 **Penguin Homes** 10

Chapter 3 **Penguin Food** 16

Chapter 4 **Penguin Nurseries** . . . 18

Chapter 5 **Penguin Parents** 28

Chapter 6 **Penguin Enemies** 36

Chapter 7 **People and Penguins** . 40

On Sharing a Book 44
A NOTE TO ADULTS

Glossary 46

Index 48

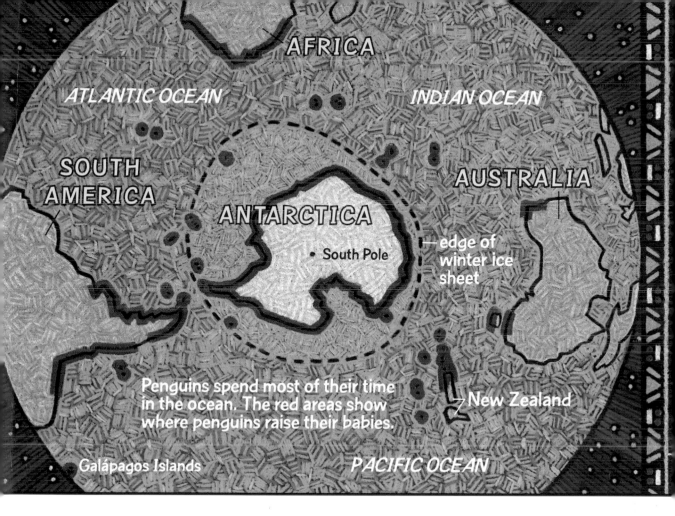

AFRICA

ATLANTIC OCEAN

INDIAN OCEAN

SOUTH
AMERICA

AUSTRALIA

ANTARCTICA

• South Pole

—edge of
winter ice
sheet

Penguins spend most of their time
in the ocean. The red areas show
where penguins raise their babies.

New Zealand

Galápagos Islands

PACIFIC OCEAN

Be a Word Detective

Can you find these words as you read about the penguin's life? Be a detective and try to figure out what they mean. You can turn to the glossary on page 46 for help.

chick	**fasting**	**predators**
colonies	**floes**	**preens**
crèche	**incubating**	**prey**
down	**molt**	

Chapter 1

Penguins are clumsy when they walk on the land. But they are good swimmers. Can penguins fly?

Penguins Are Special Birds

Penguins are amazing. They walk upright, like little people. A wet penguin looks like it's dressed in a rubber suit. But the suit is made of feathers. The little person is a bird.

Most birds can fly. But penguins can't. Penguins don't need to fly. They spend much of their lives swimming in the sea. Sometimes penguins come onto the land. But they have few enemies on the land. They don't need to fly to escape from enemies.

Sometimes penguins swim really fast. They race along, leaping in and out of the water.

This Adélie penguin looks as if it's ready to fly. But it can't fly. Its wings are much too small.

Penguins have small wings. They are useless for flying. But they are great for swimming. A penguin's wings are really flippers. A penguin has strong wing muscles. The muscles help the bird "fly" underwater. A penguin uses its tail and feet to steer.

There are 17 kinds of penguins. The kinds of penguins look much alike. They all have

Rockhopper penguins have fancy yellow feathers on their heads. These colorful feathers are called plumes.

short necks, stubby feet, and a round shape. They all have black and white feathers.

The main difference between penguins is their size. The smallest kind of penguin is the little penguin. It is about 16 inches tall and weighs less than 3 pounds. The emperor penguin is the largest penguin. It stands nearly 4 feet tall and can weigh more than 90 pounds.

Chapter 2

This is a macaroni penguin. Where do macaroni penguins live?

Penguin Homes

All penguins live south of the equator. The equator is the imaginary line around the middle of the earth. The Galápagos penguin lives near the equator. The other kinds of penguins live farther south.

Antarctica is the frozen continent at the bottom of the earth. It is the coldest place in the world. In winter, the water along the coast of Antarctica freezes into a huge sheet of ice.

Seven kinds of penguins live on or near Antarctica. Gentoo, chinstrap, Adélie (uh-DAY-lee), and emperor penguins live on the ice sheet around Antarctica. Macaroni, rockhopper, and king penguins live on islands near Antarctica.

Even in summer, most of Antarctica is covered with ice. In some places, the ice is over 1 mile thick.

The water around Antarctica is very cold. But penguins are good at staying warm. Penguins have short, stiff feathers. The feathers are waterproof. When a penguin swims, it flattens its feathers against its body. The feathers keep cold water away from the penguin's skin.

Birds who fly have long, narrow wing feathers. But penguins have short feathers on their wings. This is a chinstrap penguin.

Penguins are good at staying warm. They may get too hot, even in cold weather. Sometimes they eat snow to cool off.

When a penguin is on land, it lets its feathers stand up. Under the stiff feathers are soft, fuzzy feathers called down. The stiff feathers and the down trap warm air next to the penguin's skin.

This gentoo penguin's feathers are waterproof, so they don't get wet. The water stays on the outside.

A penguin preens to keep its feathers waterproof. When it preens, it uses its beak to clean its feathers. A penguin's body makes a special oil. Preening spreads oil on the penguin's feathers. The oil makes the feathers waterproof.

Penguins stay at sea for days or months at a time. Sometimes they climb onto floating chunks of ice called floes. Penguins rest and preen on floes. Then they slide back into the ocean.

This ice floe is floating near the shore of Antarctica. Several penguins are resting on it.

Chapter 3

These king penguins are hunting for food in the sea. What do penguins eat?

Penguin Food

All penguins are predators (PREH-duh-turz). Predators are animals who hunt other animals for food.

Penguins find their food in the ocean. They eat many kinds of small sea creatures. They eat fish, squid, and shrimplike animals called krill. The animals penguins hunt are called their prey.

Most penguins catch their prey near the surface of the ocean. But penguins also dive for food. The biggest penguins dive the deepest. The emperor penguin can dive almost the length of five football fields.

Penguins spend much of their lives at sea. But in the spring, most penguins leave the ocean. They swim to land to start families.

Krill are small animals that live in the ocean. They are related to shrimp.

Chapter 4

A penguin may have to walk more than 1 mile from the ocean to its nesting place. Most penguins nest in the spring. When does spring begin in Antarctica?

Penguin Nurseries

In Antarctica, spring begins in October. In the spring, the days are warmer. Much of the ice around Antarctica breaks up. Then penguins can swim to shore.

A penguin's nesting place may be a beach, hillside, or cliff. Penguins walk from the shore to their nesting place. Sometimes a steep, snowy hill stands in the way. Then a penguin jabs its beak into the ground and pulls itself up. To go down hills, a penguin slides on its belly.

This hill is too steep for the penguin to walk up. So it is using its beak and flippers to help it climb.

Each summer, millions of penguins come to Antarctica and nearby islands to nest.

Penguins like to be with other penguins. They nest in groups called colonies. A colony usually has only one kind of penguin. But other colonies of penguins may be nearby.

Each colony has hundreds or thousands of penguins. The penguins hiss, grunt, croak, and make trumpeting sounds. They bow, stretch, and point their beaks at the sky. These are some of the ways penguins talk with each other. Because there are so many penguins, a colony is messy, smelly, and loud.

Penguins make many different kinds of sounds. These gentoo penguins are trumpeting.

Each set of penguin parents picks a nesting spot. Penguins nest close together. But no penguin wants another penguin in its nesting spot. So the penguins squabble and fight. Usually, no one gets hurt. One penguin gives up and walks away.

These chinstrap penguins are sitting on their nests.

*Sometimes penguins steal pebbles from other penguins'
nests. The penguin at the right is squawking at a
penguin who tried to steal one of its pebbles.*

Penguin parents usually work together to
build a nest. Sometimes they can find moss,
grass, and feathers for their nests. But Antarctic
penguins often make nests of pebbles. Pebbles
are easy to find.

Emperor and king penguins don't build
nests. They lay only one egg at a time. Instead
of laying it in a nest, they hold it on their feet!

A penguin's egg must stay warm or it won't hatch. Keeping an egg warm while the baby chick grows inside it is called incubating (ING-kyuh-bay-ting).

The smaller Antarctic penguins sit on their eggs to incubate them. In about five weeks, the chicks peck through the eggshells and hatch.

Most penguins lay one or two eggs at a time. This rockhopper penguin is sitting on its eggs to keep them warm.

This king penguin is holding its egg on its feet. A flap of skin keeps the egg warm.

Emperor and king penguins must incubate their eggs for about eight weeks. They keep their eggs warm by covering them with a flap of skin. The skin keeps the top of the egg warm. And the penguin's feet keep the bottom of the egg from touching the cold ground.

Laying eggs takes a lot of energy. After a female king penguin lays her egg, she is very hungry. The male keeps the egg warm while the female goes to sea to eat.

King penguin parents take turns incubating their egg. But emperors don't take turns. After the female emperor lays her egg, she returns to the sea to eat. She will care for the chick when it hatches. The father emperor incubates the egg. He stays on land, with nothing to eat. He may go four months without eating.

Going without food is called fasting. All penguins fast sometimes. But only male emperors fast for four months at a time. Penguins lose weight when they fast. A male emperor may lose 35 pounds while he incubates his egg!

When a penguin is incubating its eggs, it goes without food. There is no food for penguins on the land.

Chapter 5

Most penguins nest in the spring. But emperor penguins nest in the winter. Their chicks hatch early in the spring. How do penguins feed their chicks?

Penguin Parents

Newly hatched penguin chicks are covered with down. They don't have waterproof feathers, so they cannot swim. They must stay on the land.

Penguin parents take turns caring for their chicks. One parent keeps the chicks warm under its feathers. The other parent goes to sea and eats. When it returns, it feeds the chicks.

Penguins feed their chicks seafood stew. It sounds good, but it's not something you would order. The adult penguin brings food from its stomach into its throat and mouth. The chicks poke their beaks into the parent's mouth to get the food.

This king penguin chick is asking its parent for food.

When penguin chicks are three to six weeks old, they are too big to be warmed by their parents. They leave the nest. From then on, the babies stay together in a group called a crèche (KRESH). The chicks huddle together in the crèche to stay warm.

Emperor penguin parents must walk many miles from their colony to the sea to hunt for food. While they are gone, the chicks huddle together to stay warm.

There may be thousands of birds in a king penguin colony. But even in a huge colony, a penguin parent can find its chick.

Penguin parents bring food to the crèche. Each chick knows its parents' voices. When a parent calls, its chick waddles over to be fed.

Young penguins know how to swim and hunt for food. Their parents don't have to teach them how.

Gentoo, chinstrap, Adélie, macaroni, and rockhopper chicks grow up quickly. They begin to grow adult feathers. When the chicks are 10 weeks old, they have a jacket of waterproof feathers. Then they can go to sea to hunt for food.

Emperor and king penguin chicks take much longer to grow up. Emperors stay in the colony until they are about five months old. King penguins stay for 10 months!

It takes 2 months for a king penguin egg to hatch. And it takes about 10 months for the chick to grow up. So it takes over a year for king parents to raise one chick!

Gentoo, chinstrap, and Adélie penguins usually raise two chicks each year. Macaroni, rockhopper, and emperor parents usually raise one chick each year. King penguins raise only two chicks every three years.

This young king penguin has lost most of its brown baby feathers. Soon it will be able to hunt for its own food.

These adult penguins are molting. They have some old feathers and some new feathers.

When the chicks are grown, their parents molt. When penguins molt, their old feathers fall out and new ones grow in. Molting takes two to four weeks. While they molt, penguins fast. They don't have a full coat of waterproof feathers, so they cannot hunt for food.

Chapter 6

King penguins and elephant seals are sharing this beach. Seals are predators. Do seals hunt penguins?

Penguin Enemies

Several kinds of seals come to Antarctic beaches. The seals are much bigger than penguins. Seals are predators. But they hunt only at sea. On land, penguins and seals ignore each other.

Most kinds of seals don't attack penguins in the ocean, either. But the leopard seal does. Leopard seals are big, quick predators. They wait in the water, close to shore. They snatch penguins who swim near them. So a penguin who is coming in from the sea must scramble ashore quickly. If it doesn't, a leopard seal might catch it.

On land, leopard seals are not very dangerous to penguins. The seals walk even more slowly than the penguins do.

Sheathbills are about 16 inches long. They look much like pigeons.

Most enemies of Antarctic penguins are birds. Giant petrels and brown skuas are large birds. They eat penguin eggs and attack penguin chicks. Gulls and sheathbills are smaller. They eat penguin eggs. But none of these birds can hurt healthy adult penguins.

The bird flying over this gentoo penguin colony is a skua. The penguins are trying to scare the skua away from their nests.

Chapter 7

Years ago, hunters came to Antarctica. They killed elephant seals for their fur and fat. Do people still hunt seals in Antarctica?

People and Penguins

Thousands of people visit Antarctic penguin colonies each year. The penguins are not afraid of people. King penguins often waddle right up to visitors.

Years ago, the only visitors to Antarctica were explorers and hunters. Many of them came to hunt fur seals and elephant seals. Hunters killed most of the fur seals and elephant seals that lived around Antarctica.

When the seals were nearly gone, people began to hunt penguins. They mainly hunted king penguins. The kings were fat, and they were easy to find. People cooked king penguins to turn their fat into oil.

People no longer hunt penguins or seals near Antarctica. There are laws to protect the creatures living there. Visitors travel to Antarctica to see penguins, not to kill them.

These people are visiting a colony of gentoo penguins.

This penguin is standing beside whale bones. Hunters killed most of the whales who once lived near Antarctica.

About 175 million penguins live near Antarctica. One reason there are so many is that there is plenty of krill for them to eat. Once there were many large whales near Antarctica. Most great whales eat krill, just as penguins do. Hunters killed most of the big whales of the Antarctic. There are fewer whales to eat krill. So there is more left for penguins.

Penguins need krill. They also need a clean ocean to swim and hunt in. The United States, Canada, and other countries are working together to keep the Antarctic clean. A clean ocean is just as important to penguins as a belly full of krill.

Antarctica is a good home for penguins.

On Sharing a Book

As you know, adults greatly influence a child's attitude toward reading. When a child sees you read, or when you share a book with a child, you're sending a message that reading is important. Show the child that reading a book together is important to you. Find a comfortable, quiet place. Turn off the television and limit other distractions, such as telephone calls.

Be prepared to start slowly. Take turns reading parts of this book. Stop and talk about what you're reading. Talk about the photographs. You may find that much of the shared time is spent discussing just a few pages. This discussion time is valuable for both of you, so don't move through the book too quickly. If the child begins to lose interest, stop reading. Continue sharing the book at another time. When you do pick up the book again, be sure to revisit the parts you have already read. Most importantly, enjoy the book!

Be a Vocabulary Detective

You will find a word list on page 5. Words selected for this list are important to the understanding of the topic of this book. Encourage the child to be a word detective and search for the words as you read the book together. Talk about what the words mean and how they are used in the sentence. Do any of these words have more than one meaning? You will find these words defined in a glossary on page 46.

What about Questions?

Use questions to make sure the child understands the information in this book. Here are some suggestions:

> What did this paragraph tell us? What does this picture show? What do you think we'll learn about next? How are penguins like other birds? How are they different? Where do penguins live? How do penguins stay warm? How do penguins keep their feathers waterproof? What do penguins eat? How do penguins go down steep hills? How do penguins keep their eggs warm? How do penguin parents feed their chicks? What do you think it's like being a penguin? What is your favorite part of the book? Why?

If the child has questions, don't hesitate to respond with questions of your own such as: What do *you* think? Why? What is it that you don't know? If the child can't remember certain facts, turn to the index.

Introducing the Index

The index is an important learning tool. It helps readers get information quickly without searching throughout the whole book. Turn to the index on page 48. Choose an entry, such as feathers, and ask the child to use the index to find out how feathers help penguins stay warm. Repeat this exercise with as many entries as you like. Ask the child to point out the differences between an index and a glossary. (The index helps readers find information quickly, while the glossary tells readers what words mean.)

Where in the World?

Many plants and animals found in the Early Bird Nature Books series live in parts of the world other than the United States. Encourage the child to find the places mentioned in this book on a world map or globe. Take time to talk about climate, terrain, and how you might live in such places.

All the World in Metric!

Although our monetary system is in metric units (based on multiples of 10), the United States is one of the few countries in the world that does not use the metric system of measurement. Here are some conversion activities you and the child can do using a calculator:

WHEN YOU KNOW:	MULTIPLY BY:	TO FIND:
miles	1.609	kilometers
feet	0.3048	meters
inches	2.54	centimeters
gallons	3.787	liters
pounds	0.454	kilograms

Activities

Penguins use oil to make their feathers waterproof. You can use the wax in your crayons to make paper waterproof. Use a pencil to draw two penguins on a piece of watercolor or drawing paper. Color only one of the penguins in with crayons. Color hard, and don't leave any spaces blank. Now sprinkle three or four drops of water on each penguin. What happens to the water?

Visit a zoo to see penguins. How are penguins similar to other birds in the zoo and how are they different?

Glossary

chick—a baby penguin

colonies—groups of penguins nesting together

crèche (KRESH)—young penguins who stay together for warmth while their parents are away

down—soft, fluffy feathers

fasting—going without food

floes—large sheets of floating ice

incubating (ING-kyuh-bay-ting)—keeping eggs warm so they'll hatch

molt—to lose feathers so new ones can grow in

predators (PREH-duh-turz)—animals who hunt and eat other animals

preens—cleans and smooths feathers with a beak

prey—animals who are hunted and eaten by other animals

Index

Pages listed in **bold** type refer to photographs.

chicks, 24, 26, 28–34

eggs, 23–27
enemies, 7, 36–39, 41

feathers, **9**, 12–14,
 28, 32, **34**, 35
fighting, 22, **23**
food, 16–17, 26–27,
 29, **30**, 31, 32, **34**,
 35, 42

growing up, 32–33

kinds of penguins,
 8–9, 11

location, 10–11, 15

nesting, 18–27, **28**

people and penguins,
 40–43

size, 9
staying warm, 12–13
swimming, **6**, 7, 8,
 17, **32**

voice, 21

wings, 8, **12**